PETER SUTHERLAND

SMALL TOWN KIDS NEED SOMETHING TO DO

Lichen Books

978-1-7396697-3-7

Introduction by Francesca Gavin In the late 17th Century, British writer-philosophers John Dennis, Anthony Ashley-Cooper and Edmund Burke developed the concept of connecting the sublime with aesthetics. They were particularly inspired by the beauty of Alpine nature, which they felt had a texture existing on the edge of horror and despair. This dramatic sense of infinity and beauty in nature became a dominant motif in the coming century. Peter Sutherland's multimedia works – perhaps unintentionally – play with some of this ideology. His images highlight the overwhelming, beautiful and at times terrifying qualities of nature. His work can be seen as a contemporary take on the sublime.

When Sutherland was 23 he was gifted a film camera. Processing the recent death of his father, he redirected his grief into a burst of productivity, building a body of work within weeks. He put together these new images into a self-made free publication. This first set of images led to his work being published in Vice magazine. He was soon was given the opportunity to exhibit at Rivington Arms gallery – at the time one of the Lower East Side's most lauded locations. Sutherland learned his craft without much training, making his name in magazine contributions and campaigns for streetwear brands. However, his work never felt purely commercial. He was always an artist carving out his own path.

Sutherland was raised in Colorado and spent over 20 years in New York City. His return to Colorado in 2020 with his family started a new chapter for him and his work. His personal, editorial and commercial work often comes out of autobiographical experiences; yet somehow Sutherland's work doesn't feel entirely ego-driven. It demonstrates the beauty and sweetness of the everyday life cycle. His aesthetic is raw, unpolished, accidental, and somehow alive - like the nature that surrounds him.

Although much of this work brought together in this book was created a decade ago, it exposes the ongoing tropes in the photographer's work. An awareness of the elements and the awe of the grand landscapes. He acknowledges humanity's effects to the world around him, and in his imagery the borders between human and nature overlap and spill out. He highlights how we still heavily inhabit, relate and rely on the world around us.

Collage is an ongoing technique for Sutherland, who often works with images layered in plexiglass frames and printed with inkjet on vinyl. His approach is linear and scrapbook-like; rectangles overlaying over rectangles; semi-transparencies allowing things to embrace each other. You can see the roots of that process here with his early experiments with printing on perforated mesh. In our ever-evolving minds, exact moments in our memories can lack definition. Yet the blur and the lucidity of Sutherland's montages brings us one step closer to understanding the human experience.

Francesca Gavin Lets talk about the images you've brought together here. Is it all exhibition documentation? **Peter Sutherland** So, all those works are actually from 2013, 14 and 15. I had sort of given up on the idea of making work that would ever be collected in a way or worth money in the art world. Then by chance, I did a residency with this group of artists that were 10 years younger than me. They had a studio/gallery space in Red Hook and a collective. **Francesca Gavin** This is Still House. I remember this moment in time in New York. **Peter Sutherland** It really was an organic thing. These artists were mostly from LA. I started selling my work through them and it was just a lot of fun. It was 18 months where there was a lot happening. **Francesca Gavin** It seemed to seep away after that. I suppose it's the logistics of that building? **Peter Sutherland** I'd always really wanted to crack the art world and didn't know how to do it. I always tried to do it with photography, and I watched peers like Ryan McGinley do it. But with SH, it was like the little fairy tale - just the feeling of the buzz, right? All these people were coming to Red Hook to see their work. They had a residency program within their space. For three months I did that with them. There was a group show and I was in it. Leo DiCaprio was at the opening - and then like five minutes later, someone comes up and they're like, "Leo just bought your piece. You've got to come meet him." And I was like, "Oh geez." It was just a lot of fun, basically. We're still friends now. Some of them have gone on to do different things; some are still making art. **Francesca Gavin** I originally discovered your work from style magazines and the underground culture scene. Placing that work within an art context is really interesting. How do you transition is a fundamental discussion I've had with a lot of people over the years. It's still you, essentially. **Peter Sutherland** Yeah, I mean a lot of people have done it starting from a graffiti background or from skateboarding, but for some reason, there's a different sensibility within the art world. **Francesca Gavin** Tell me more about the works. **Peter Sutherland** That work uses perforated window decals. It's mesh that they use for advertising. You see it in advertising that goes over windows, like on a bus. I don't even know if they use it in the UK or Europe, but in the States they do. These works are all printed on that material. You can see through the perforated holes in the image, to see what's is below it, in this case the plywood chipboard. It is inherently a bit about photography in a way, where you are using pinholes to let light through. That's interesting to me. It was a fun analogue way to create a Photoshop effect. And specifically using nature imagery over that type of wood. What do you guys call it? It's called OSB (oriented strand board), it's like the really cheap kind of wood used for construction. **Francesca Gavin** Plywood? MDF? **Peter Sutherland** Yeah. I like that contrast of seeing really pristine images of nature up against super mulched down construction-grade level material. It tied back to all my work. I've always been interested in this crux of nature and humankind. In 2006, I did this book of deer photos - in like parking lots and stuff. Kind of sad, kind of humorous. You see the past, present, future in this one image. I've always been into work that kind of continues that narrative. **Francesca Gavin** I'm remembering that you did a series of prints of solar flares for Printed Matter, that play with the same thing but in a really simplified way. They're obvi-ously nature but very much obviously about photography. **Peter Sutherland** Yeah. It's nature, but they've gone through this photo process. Again, that's a simple thing. All it is is cropping in. Everyone can relate to those because everyone's had a role or a photo that comes back with a flare on it. **Francesca Gavin** I know you've moved back to Colorado, the state you grew up in. The photographic imagery in this book has this big, elemental sense of nature. You were already kind of looking beyond just an urban context. **Peter Sutherland** I feel like a lot of artists I've known over the years have done that in New York. They have something that's on their mind that they bring with them from somewhere else. Even Harmony Korine - he has made so much work about Tennessee… **Francesca Gavin** Where were your images taken? Like, was it over a period of time or during their residency? I'm assuming they weren't taken in Red Hook! **Peter Sutherland** Some of them are like in the Olympic Peninsula and Washington State. Some of the mountain ones were taken in Nepal. And some of the bonfires, we just made.

Francesca Gavin **What do you find interesting about travel being part of your process?** *Peter Sutherland* I definitely get inspired by films and traveling. I could watch one film and think about everything that went into it. Film is sight, sound, you know, editing, casting, score - so much that goes into a film. If I even, you know, stay one night somewhere new, I always see something interesting. Ironically enough, I really don't like getting on planes. Like I'll do it, but it really scares me. Maybe I did it too much. I don't know… but I'm definitely always inspired by traveling and seeing new things. I know that's a privilege. It doesn't always have to be somewhere exotic. *Francesca Gavin* **What films are you inspired by at the moment?** *Peter Sutherland* It doesn't have to be an artful movie. The production itself can be impressive. I saw this movie 'Gimme Shelter', a Maysles Brothers documentary about The Rolling Stones. For some reason, that movie was a really big deal for me. Because there's so much in this one film - life and death and sadness and love and hope. There's the Hells Angels fighting with people in the crowd. There's chaos and it's edited into this like symphony kind of movie. That and then there's 'The Lost Boys', which I also love. *Francesca Gavin* **Great soundtrack.** *Peter Sutherland* 'Magnolia' - I really love that movie. It doesn't have to be specific directors or anything. It's just more kind of the feat and the scale of what goes into making a movie and making it work. Movies have a special place. Do you know, the Safdie Brothers in New York? They started with short films and now they have films with huge stars, but they're still indie and they're really interesting. They made a movie called 'Heaven Knows What' and 'Good Time'. *Francesca Gavin* **You've made a narrative-based short film 'Curb Heads', too?** *Peter Sutherland* 'Curb Heads' was a personal film, shot where I grew up, about two hours from here. I love when things are organic. All the kids in that film are my friends' sons and their friends. That was a really cool experience. I also learned how hard it is to make basic dialogue work. I had written a little script and none of it sounded real when we were trying to shoot it. *Francesca Gavin* **Looking at your photographs - or at least the ones in this book - there are no figures, which seems intentional.** *Peter Sutherland* I had gotten a little bit frustrated with the limitations of photography. White chrome or black frame horizontal. I love all that stuff. Portraiture, landscape, lifestyle like all those things. But really from 2010 on, I was really interested in trying to do something else and push it a little bit. If you look at photography, it's a little bit strict. But art is anything. Turn it upside down and light it on fire, break in half, make it on any material. Make a quilt if you want, like, whatever. I was also trying to find refined images that would last, I guess. They're just kind of classic nature images. *Francesca Gavin* **It's really hard to depict mountains without dealing with like the weight of Ansel Adams or the heritage of the giant American landscape on your shoulders. Were you twisting or thinking about that at all?** *Peter Sutherland* When I look at that kind of work, a lot of it feels like scenic, like a long exposure of a waterfall. That secondary part of the process, printing it on mesh and laying it over something, felt like it changed it enough. I wasn't thinking about Ansel Adams. I like John Divola a lot, and Walker Evans. *Francesca Gavin* **A lot of the pieces seem quite large. A single image turned into a triptych, for example.** *Peter Sutherland* I felt like these dots and holes was almost like what you could get from painting - where if you look at it close or if from 15 steps back, it looks completely different? Photographers don't really get to do that as much, because even if I make something big, they're still just looking at a little bit of grain. Up close, they almost become kind of abstract, and then when you get further away, they look different and then also the way the two layers bounce off each other really worked at scale. Sometimes you're seeing the plywood more than the image. The other thing that's kind of interesting about those images is you see the wood the most in the parts that are black - which is counterintuitive in a way. You'd think that would be the most prominent. That played into the scale for me. *Francesca Gavin* **What camera do you use?** *Peter Sutherland* I use pretty basic 35mm film cameras, usually, but I'm not really picky. I just like them to work, because at this point, they're all fragile antiques. It's like a battle to keep those things up and running.

The Dude Ranch, 2014
4' × 6', OSB, inkjet on perforated vinyl, matte medium

Next:
The Law of Reversed Effect, 2014
8' × 12' 5", OSB, inkjet on perforated vinyl, matte medium

Previous:
The Law of Reversed Effect 2, 2014
8' × 12' 5", OSB, inkjet on perforated vinyl, matte medium

Opposite:
The Least Hazy Part of the Year, 2014
4' × 6', OSB, inkjet on perforated vinyl, matte medium

The Mountain Chrome, 2014
4' × 6', inkjet on perforated vinyl, masonite, india ink, enamel, stickers, matte medium

The News in Ireland, 2014
4' × 6', inkjet on perforated vinyl, masonite, india ink,
packing tape, stickers, matte medium

The Potential of Your Roommates, 2014
4' × 6', inkjet on perforated vinyl, masonite, india ink,
stickers, matte medium

The Salt Flats, 2014
4' × 6', inkjet on perforated vinyl, masonite, india ink,
enamel, stickers, matte medium

The Sphinx Moth, 2014
4' × 6', inkjet on perforated vinyl, masonite, india ink,
enamel, stickers, matte medium

SPHINX MOTHS (HUMMINGBIRD OR HAWK MOTHS)

Sphinx Moths are medium-sized to large, heavy bodied moths with long narrow front wings sometimes extending 5" or more. They are strong fliers & fly with a very rapid wing beat (some up to 40 mph.) Many are mistaken for the hummingbird, because they hover over exotic plants reaching down deep into the flower with their proboscis. This proboscis can extend up to 12" or more on some Sphinx Moths. Some of these moths rob beehives. The bees seem unable to stop them because of the draft caused by their rapidly moving wings. Some Sphinx Moths are day fliers, but most are active at dusk or twilight.

DEATH'S HEAD SPHINX MOTH (see arrows to right)

The Death's Head Sphinx Moth is found in Southern & Central Europe and on the British Isles.
In the rest position the moth folds its wings horizontally over its body. The pattern on its back is great resemblance of a death's head.

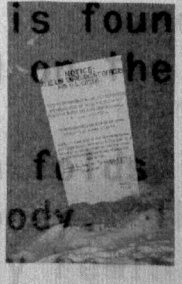

MAY NATURAL HISTORY

These Are Progressive Years, 2014
4' × 6', OSB, inkjet on perforated vinyl, matte medium

This is Patagucci, 2014
4' × 6', OSB, inkjet on perforated vinyl, matte medium

This One is Also Good, 2014
4' × 6', masonite, acrylic, decals

Tropical Deep Woods Off, 2014
4' × 6', OSB, inkjet on perforated vinyl, matte medium

Trust Fall Fail, 2014
4' × 6', OSB, inkjet on perforated vinyl, matte medium

Trust Fall, 2014
4' × 6', OSB, inkjet on perforated vinyl, matte medium

Previous:
When Sun Screen Goes in Your Eyes, 2014
8' × 12' 5", OSB, inkjet on perforated vinyl, matte medium

Opposite:
No Masters Only Experts, 2014
4' × 6', inkjet on perforated vinyl, masonite, india ink,
enamel, stickers, matte medium

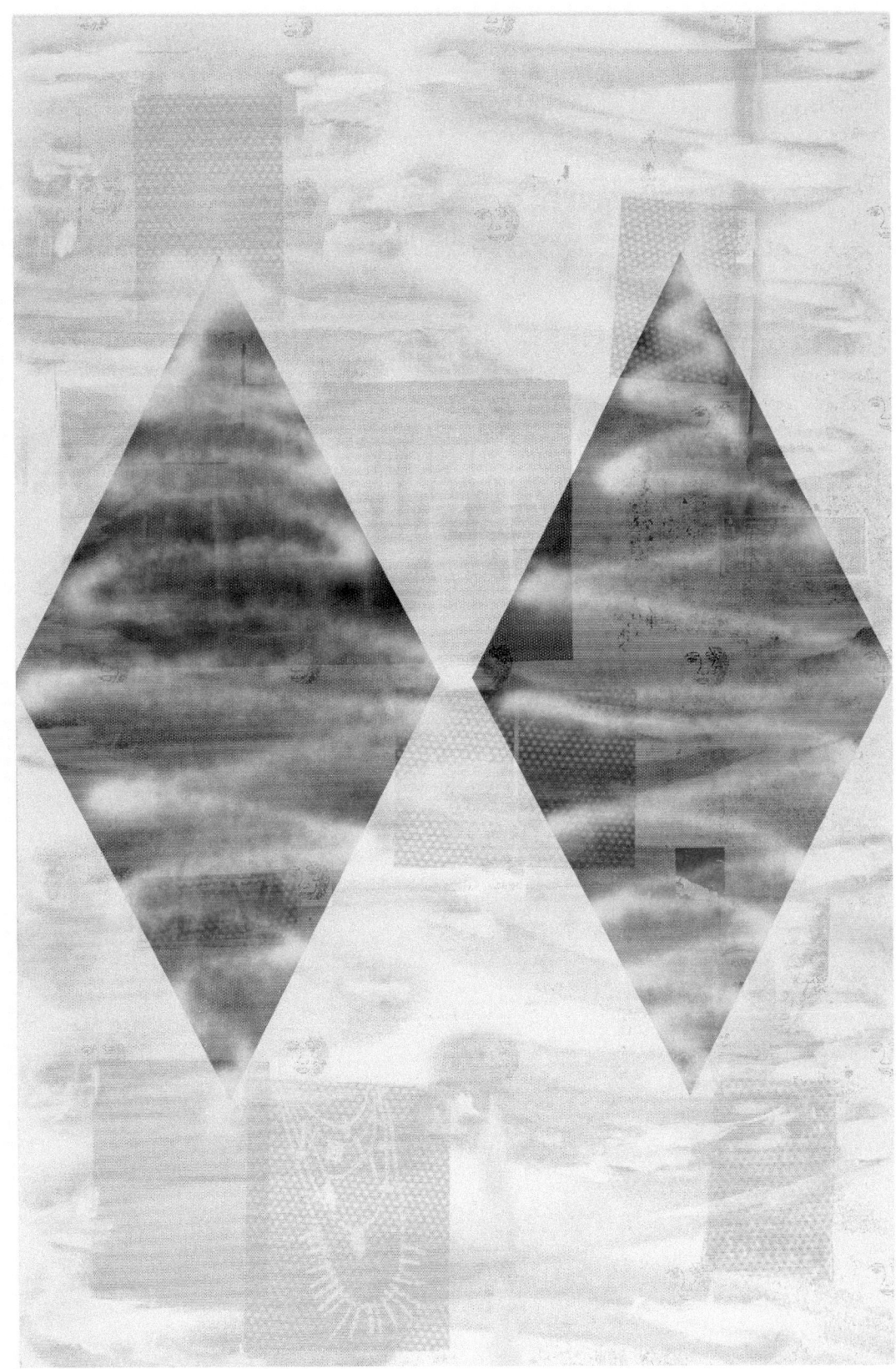

Over 40 and Loving it, 2014
4' × 6', inkjet on perforated vinyl, masonite, india ink,
enamel, stickers, matte medium

P+A+L+M+S, 2014
11" × 28", cut stone, inkjet on perforated vinyl

Paradise Found 2, 2014
4' × 6', OSB, inkjet on perforated vinyl, matte medium

Questionable Judgement, 2015
3' × 5', aluminium, inkjet on perforated vinyl

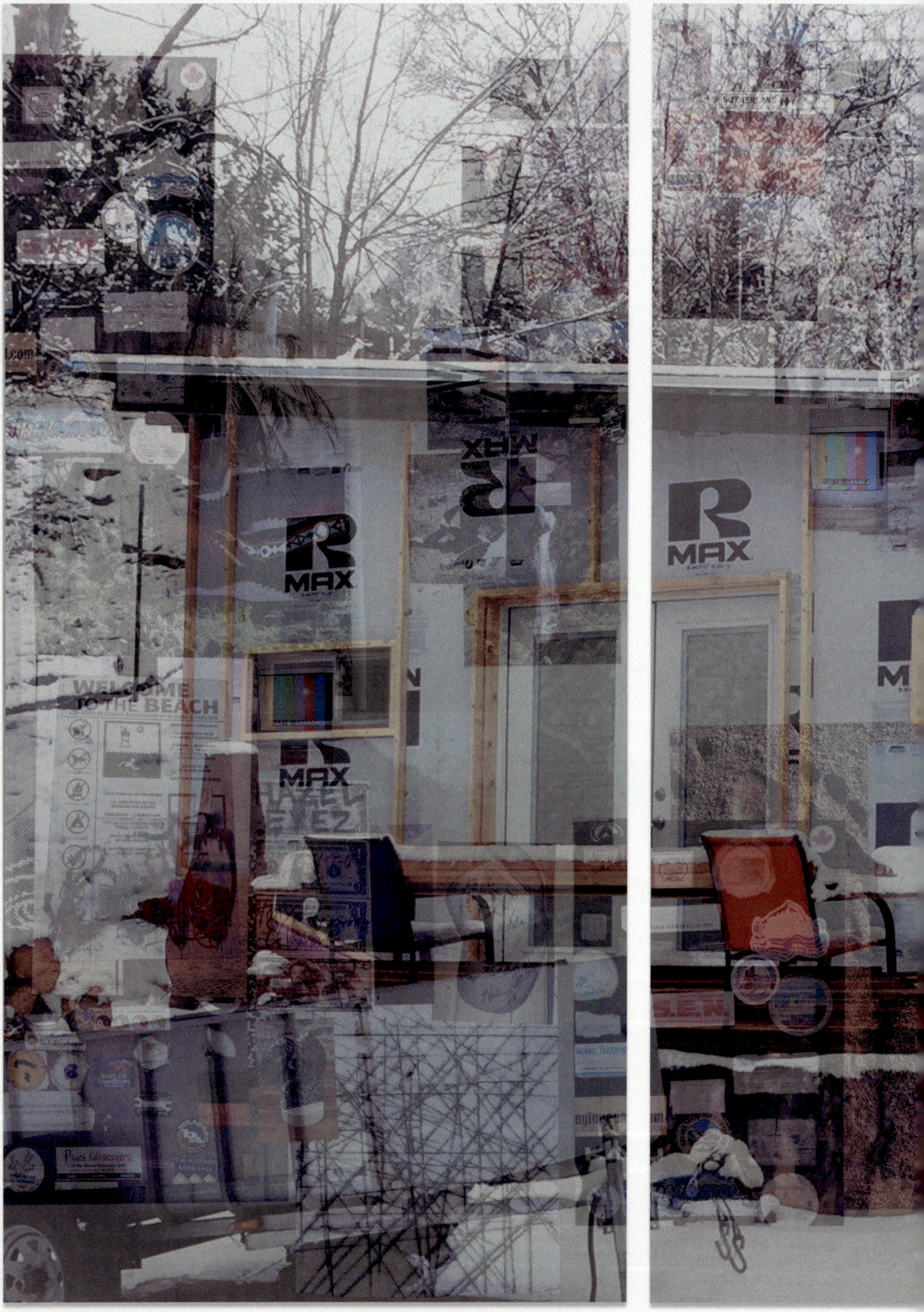

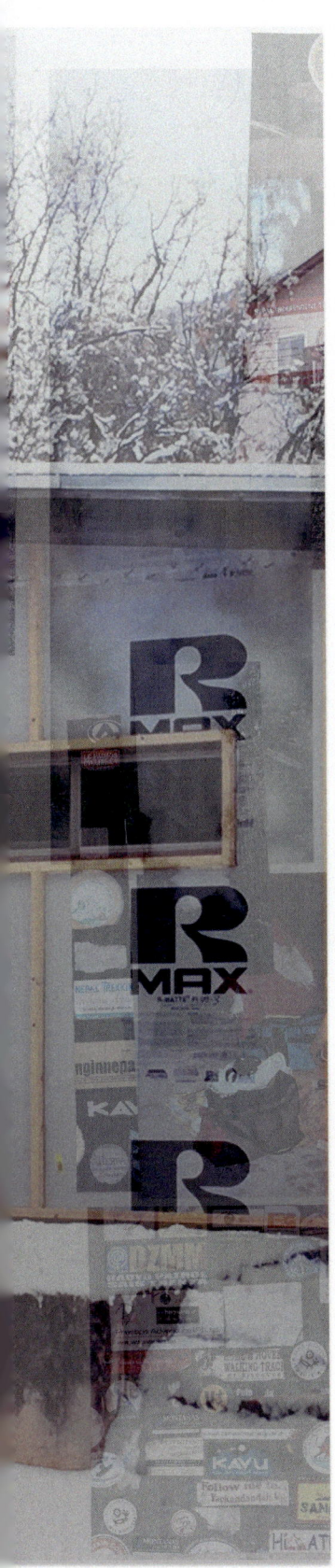

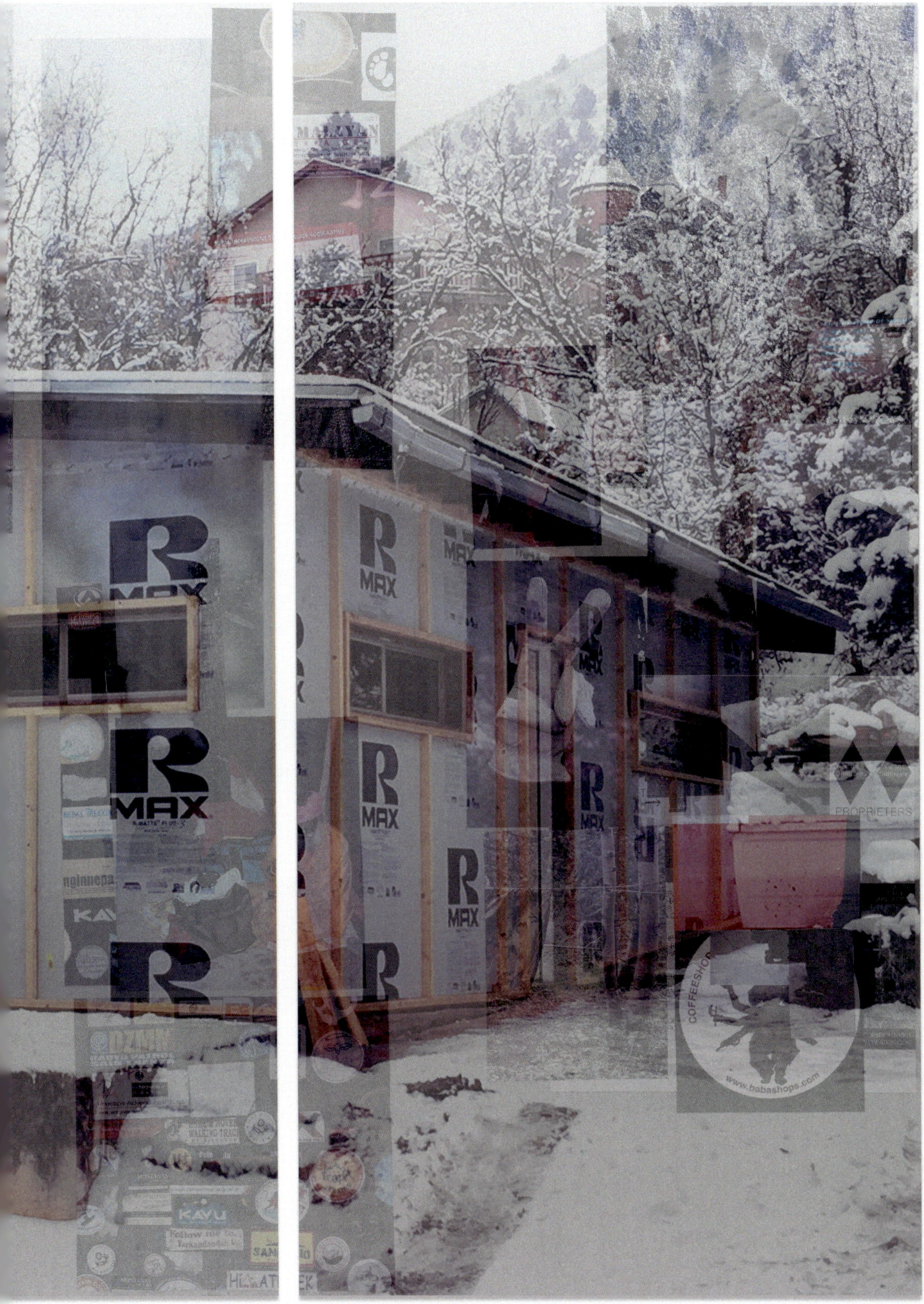
R MAX
PROPRIETERS
COFFEESHOP
www.babashops.com
KAVU

Previous:
Recognized Within the Community, 2015
8' × 10', masonite, aluminium, cintra, decals,
inkjet on perforated vinyl, matte medium

Opposite:
Reunion Tour, 2014
4' × 6', OSB, inkjet on perforated vinyl, matte medium

Previous:
Reverb in the Valley, 2014
8' × 12' 5", OSB, inkjet on perforated vinyl, matte medium

Opposite:
Siberian Huskies Are Cool, 2014
4' × 6', OSB, inkjet on perforated vinyl, matte medium

Singed Eyebrows, 2014
4' × 6', OSB, inkjet on perforated vinyl, matte medium

Slammed and Tinted, 2014
4' × 6', inkjet on perforated vinyl, masonite, india ink,
enamel, stickers, matte medium

Small Town Kids Need Something to Do, 2014
4' × 6', OSB, inkjet on perforated vinyl, matte medium

We Are the Elders, 2014
4' × 6', inkjet on perforated vinyl, masonite, india ink,
enamel, stickers, matte medium

Welcome to College, 2014
4' × 6', inkjet on perforated vinyl, masonite, india ink, enamel, stickers, matte medium

Previous:
West Coast Therapy Cot, 2013
6' × 2' × 2", sublimated print on canvas, store bought cot

Opposite:
Wet Web, 2014
4' × 6', OSB, inkjet on perforated vinyl, matte medium

Where Are You Going to Spend Eternity, 2014
4' × 6', OSB, inkjet on perforated vinyl, matte medium

Where Guitars Come From, 2014
4' × 6', OSB, inkjet on perforated vinyl, matte medium

Wilderness of Pain, 2014
2' × 3', OSB, inkjet on perforated vinyl, matte medium

Yoga Teacher Gone Wild, 2014
4' × 6', OSB, inkjet on perforated vinyl, matte medium

You're an Inspiration to Us All, 2014
4' × 6', OSB, inkjet on perforated vinyl, matte medium

Next:
From the Mountain to the Mesa, 2014
8' × 12' 5", OSB, inkjet on perforated vinyl, matte medium

Previous:
Glacier Glasses View, 2014
8' × 12' 5", OSB, inkjet on perforated vinyl, matte medium

Opposite:
Happy Can-Per, 2014
4' × 6', inkjet on perforated vinyl, masonite, india ink, stickers, matte medium

Heated Driveway, 2014
4' × 6', OSB, inkjet on perforated vinyl, matte medium

Heated Seats, 2014
4' × 6', OSB, inkjet on perforated vinyl, matte medium

Highlands 3, 2014
4' × 6', OSB, inkjet on perforated vinyl, matte medium

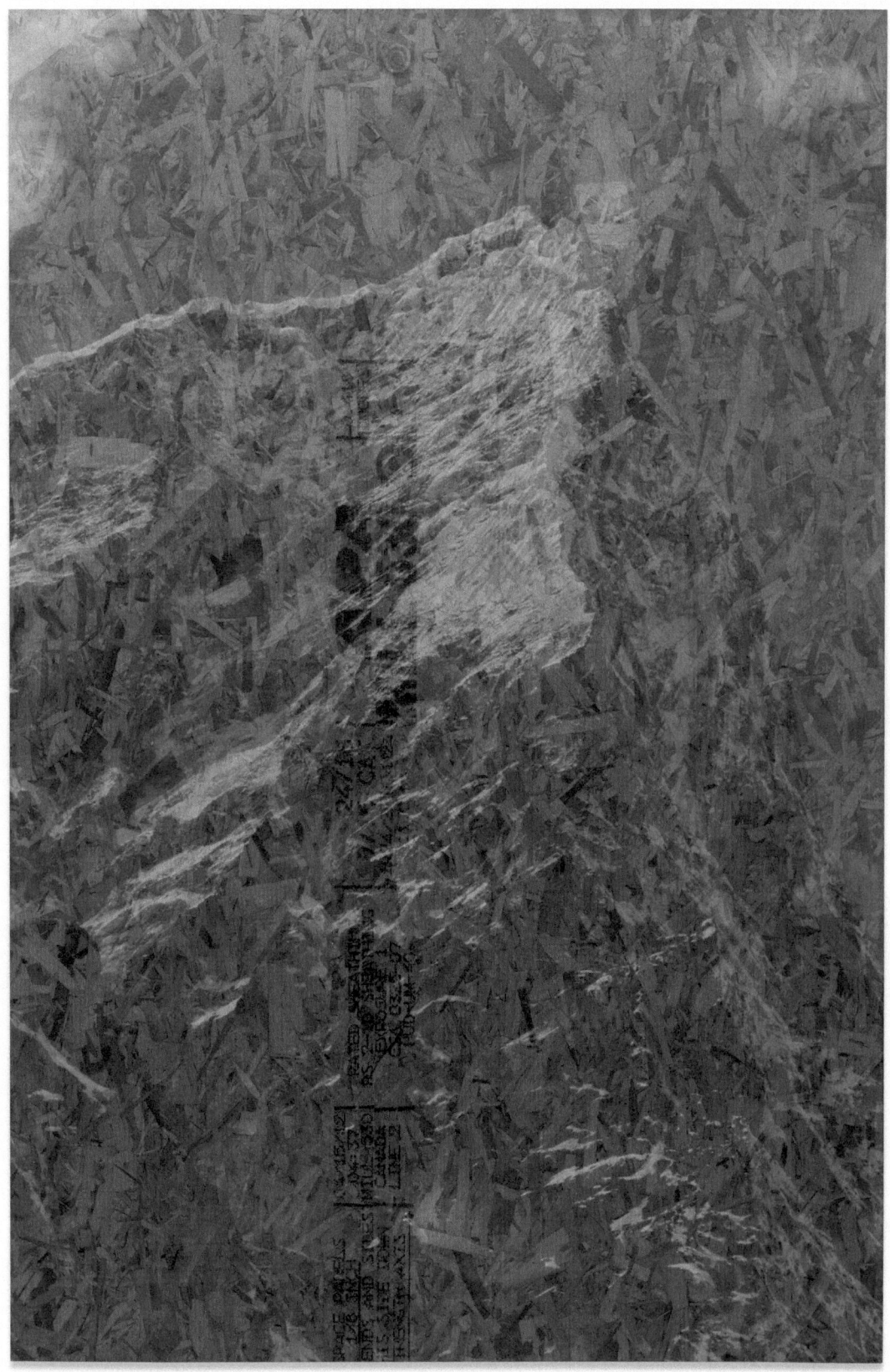

Highlands, 2014
4' × 6', OSB, inkjet on perforated vinyl, matte medium

Hittin' the Dusty Trail, 2014
4' × 6', inkjet on perforated vinyl, masonite, enamel, stickers, matte medium

I Follow Sports, 2014
4' × 6', decals, perforated decals, matte medium on masonite, spray paint

I Tried Rock Climbing Once, 2014
4' × 6', decals, perforated decals, matte medium
on masonite, spray paint, screws

Next:
In the Beginning, 2014
8' × 12' 5", OSB, inkjet on perforated vinyl, matte medium

Previous:
Kalar Pata Nepal, 2014
8' × 12' 5", OSB, inkjet on perforated vinyl, matte medium

Opposite:
Less Haters at the Equator, 2014
2' × 3', OSB, inkjet on perforated vinyl, matte medium

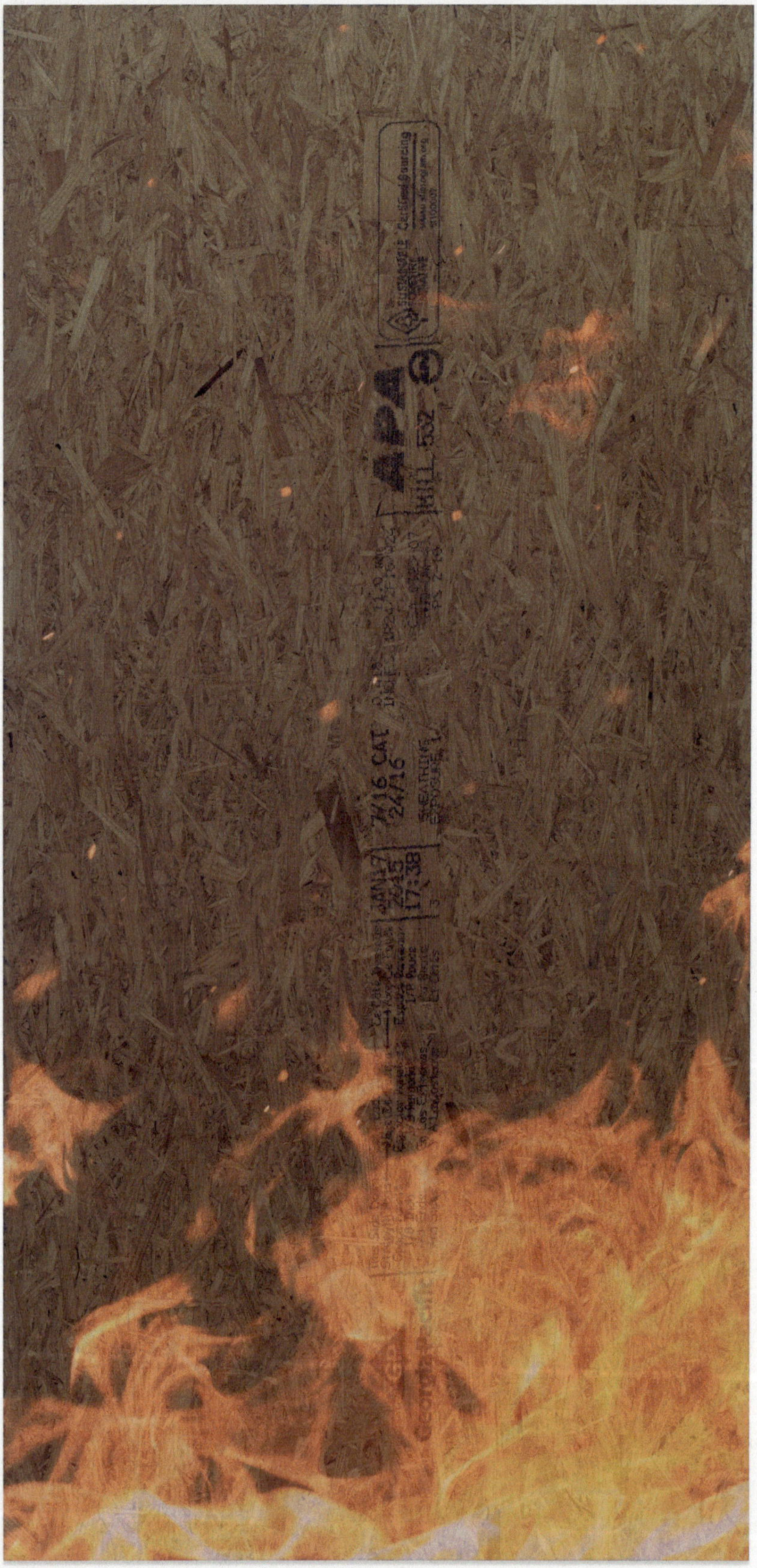

Previous:
Lifetime Achievement Award, 2014
8' × 12' 5", OSB, inkjet on perforated vinyl, matte medium

Opposite:
Look Out of Any Window, 2014
4' × 6', OSB, inkjet on perforated vinyl, matte medium

Many Moons (and Suns), 2014
4' × 6', inkjet on perforated vinyl, masonite, india ink,
enamel, stickers, matte medium

Summer Jam Tickets, 2014
4' × 6', OSB, inkjet on perforated vinyl, matte medium

The Aging Skater, 2014
4' × 6', OSB, inkjet on perforated vinyl, matte medium

The Casino and the Campground, 2014
4' × 6', inkjet on perforated vinyl, masonite, stickers,
matte medium

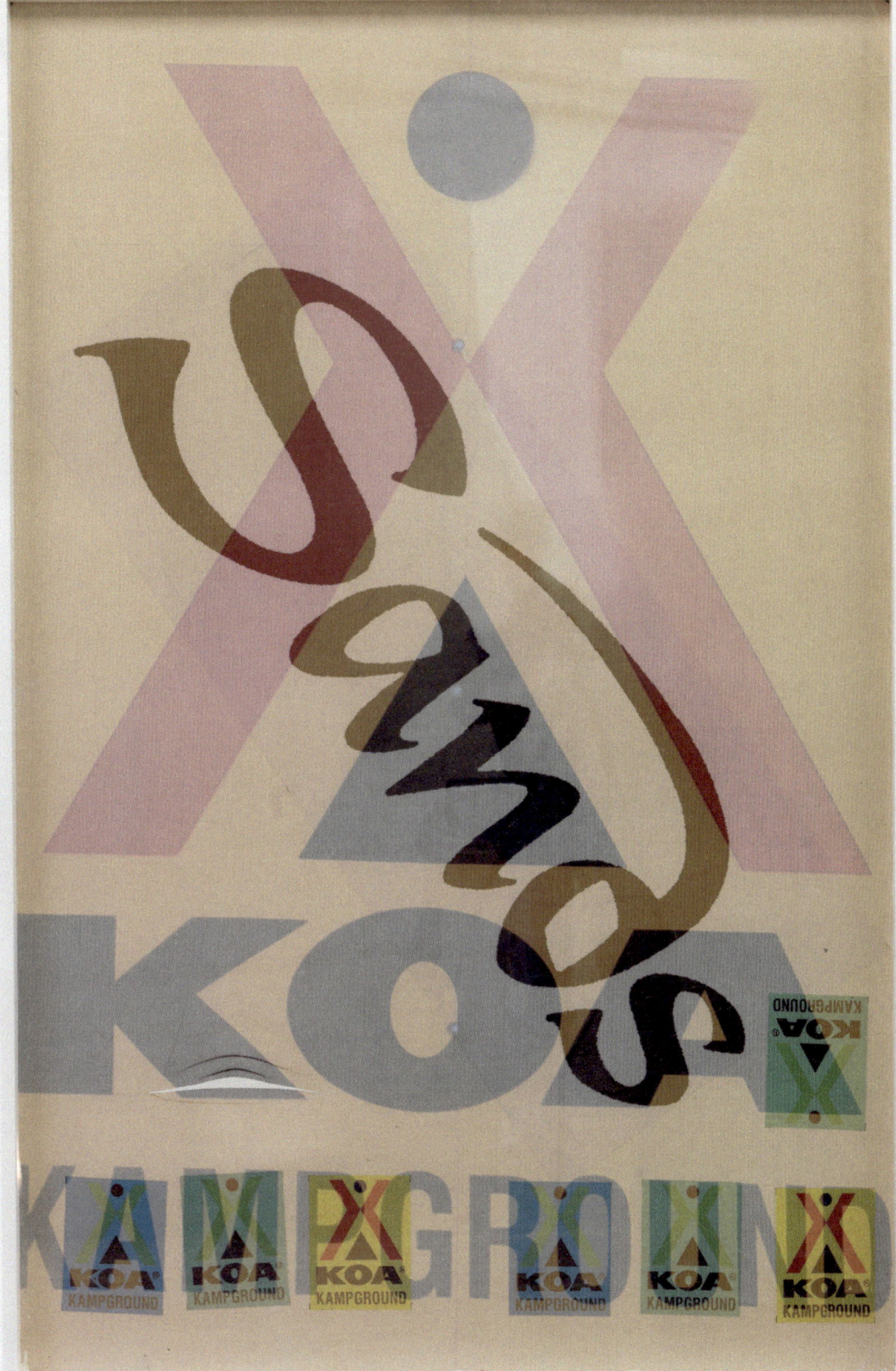

Under Bright Skies, 2014
4' × 6', inkjet on perforated vinyl, india ink, stickers,
matte medium on masonite

Next:
One Bar of Service, 2015, NY
Installation view, Stillhouse Gallery, Red Hook

Previous:
A Dedication to a Tribute of a Monument, 2014
8' × 8', OSB, inkjet on perforated vinyl, matte medium

Opposite:
A Reason to Wear Ridiculous Gear, 2014
4' × 6', inkjet on perforated vinyl, masonite, enamel, stickers, matte medium

Previous:
A Screenshot of a Jpeg, 2014, Nepal
8' × 12' 5", OSB, inkjet on perforated vinyl, matte medium

Opposite:
Alien vs. Perpetrator, 2014
2' × 3', OSB, inkjet on perforated vinyl, matte medium

Austrian Solstice, 2014
4' × 6', OSB, inkjet on perforated vinyl, matte medium

Bonfire 7, 2014
4' × 6', OSB, inkjet on perforated vinyl, matte medium

Previous:
Calling Your Friends By Their Nicknames, 2014
4' × 6', OSB, inkjet on perforated vinyl, matte medium

Opposite:
Canadian Tuxedo, 2014
4' × 6', OSB, inkjet on perforated vinyl, matte medium

Class of '94, 2014
4' × 6', OSB, inkjet on perforated vinyl, matte medium

Deep Free Deep Woods Off, 2014
4' × 6', OSB, inkjet on perforated vinyl, matte medium

Double Fried, 2014
4' × 6', OSB, inkjet on perforated vinyl, matte medium

Eternally Flamed, 2014
4' × 6', OSB, inkjet on perforated vinyl, matte medium

For DJ, 2014, Nepal
4' × 6', OSB, inkjet on perforated vinyl, matte medium

Peter Sutherland would like to thank the
Stillhouse Group for their support and friendship.

All images © Peter Sutherland
Text by Francesca Gavin
Design by All Purpose
Printed by Jelgavas Tipogrāfija

Published by Lichen Books, 2023
First Edition of 500

© Lichen Books 2023
lichen-books.org

ISBN 978-1-7396697-3-7

All efforts have been made to ensure copyrighted images are used
with permission, and referenced correctly.

All rights reserved. No parts of this publication may be reproduced
or transmitted, in any form or by any means, electronic or mechanical,
including photocopying, recording, or any other information storage
or retrieval system without prior permission of the publisher.